Numerology: Practical Guide to Mastering Numerology - Learn How to Take Control of Your Destiny, Identify Strengths & Weaknesses, and Discover Who You

Really Are and Your Real Purpose

by Cassandra Meek

All Rights Reserved. No part of this publication may be reproduced in any form or by any means, including scanning, photocopying, or otherwise without prior written permission of the copyright holder. Copyright ©
Mysterious Ways Publishing Co. 2015

Table of Contents

Introduction

Numerology And It's Different Aspect

What Can Numerology Do For You

How Numerology Works

How To Do Simple Numerology

Meaning of The Numbers

Importance of Name and Birth Date

Unique Abilities of The Numbers

The Lesson That Each Number Presents
Master Numbers
Conclusion

Introduction

Numerology is the art of foreseeing the future with the help of numbers. It mainly deals with the birth number of an individual. The existence of Numerology is age old. There are many incidents when an individuals' future has been predicted by calculating his/her birth number. In fact over the years, the numerologists have calculated the birth time and birth number of famous personalities to show how their birth number had changed the course of their life and in turn the History of Mankind.

Your Date of Birth is a Doorway in Time:

If there is any moment that can be pinpointed as an individual's total transformation then it was the moment of his birth. The moment they were born, they made the transition to a new reality – the reality of a human life. And he/she left behind his/her past life, completely oblivious of whom they were and entered this realm in the purest form where they are untouched by judgment, material wealth, stress, tension, expectations and concepts as well.

Yet, in that moment, the individual was still a human who possessed an unique character something very similar to one's DNA. Everything existed in its true potential, waiting to be explored – just like a play which is about to begin.

The word relatively was coined by Albert Einstein. However before this word came into existence everything was deemed to be the way they were. No one assume that, there can be something like relativity where the interpretation of situations/things/occurrences and time will varies from one individual to another. But the moment this word was gained and it received accreditation all the world over, our perceptions and beliefs changed forever. This term awakened new ideas and possibilities were unheard or unthoughtful-of. Our spiritual horizon widened and we became aware of different aspects of life.

The same kind of change occurred when numerology was introduced. The language of numbers had a profound impact on all other kinds of language and our interpretation of things began to change. We became aware of personal traits and characteristics and how every individual is different and how our Life path Number determines our course of action.

How you will react to the different incidents and scenarios in your life – all will be guided by your birth number. Your birth number is highly detrimental as far as your course of action is concerned. In this book, we have dealt with Numerology in depth so that your concepts are completely cleared and you have a better informed idea about this subject.

Numerology is not something to be taken lightly because our birth number ultimately determines who we will be.

Following are the different chapters that have been dealt with in this book:

- **What is Numerology**
    - What is Numerology?
    - Where did it originate, how has it progressed in the present day
    - Who were the Fathers of numerology, and who have been the major contributors

- **What Can Numerology Do For You (The Benefits)**

- **How Numerology Works**
    - Gives examples of how to work with the numbers, with simple addition, and sometimes subtraction.
    - How to convert letters of the alphabet to number

- **Meaning of the Numbers**
    - Discusses the importance of the name you were given at birth, and the importance of your date of birth.
    - Numbers can be used as a positive expression, and as a negative expression

- **Unique Abilities of the Numbers**
    - Relationships and how the numbers work in relationships

- o The lesson that each number presents.

- **Master Numbers**
  - o How master numbers are obtained, and what they mean
  - o How master numbers bring special challenges and rewards
  - o Master numbers can mean possible great things to come in the future
  - o Master numbers may be a gift or a curse.

Note: The above mentioned 6 chapters and their sub divisions have been dealt in a simple, lucid way for the better understanding of the reader.

Numerology And It's Different Aspect

Numerology is the art of foreseeing the future with the help of numbers. In other words we can say that numerology is a culmination of different beliefs in different fields like the divine, mystical or other interesting relations between a number and interesting happenings. There are many beliefs and systems surround this branch of study. In the early ages the mathematicians made use of numerology but gradually over the years they got separated from mathematics and were associated with pseudo-mathematics or pseudo-science by modern scientists.

The magnificence of using numbers with human characteristic is that they are naturally and inherently connected. There is nothing inconsistent in adding the number 1 with that of origin or invention simply because no matter what is the type of language opted for, number 1 will always be the beginning, the start and the numero uno.

WHAT IS NUMEROLOGY?

The symbolism of numbers is called Numerology. The number is sued to determine and individual's personality, talents, strength, weakness, obstacles, dealing with others and emotional reactions as well. Numerologists take your birth number to chart out your life and how you can take advantage of the unexplored opportunities. In other words, in a simpler language, numerology can be referred to as a tool that will help you understand the different equations of life so that you can handle the different situations in an apt way and maintain a proper relationship with your loved ones. When you have your life chart in front of you, you will be better prepared to face the different situations and handle them in the apt way.

Numerology has a higher practical application than any other mode of understanding human characteristics and traits because each individual has a specific number and that number will give you an inner insight in to your nature, traits, talents and the different challenges and obstacles that will be thrown at you by life in the years that are to come. In fact it will act as a guide and will tell you about the different opportunities and obstacles so that you are well prepared to handle them in the best possible way. In the ultimate analysis it will depend on the particular individual whether he will make use of it or not.

WHERE DID IT ORIGINATE? HOW HAS IT PROGRESSED IN THE PRESENT DAY?

If you flip through the pages of history you will see that some 10,000 years ago, Numerology grew its roots in Egypt and Babylonia. In fact the Hebrews developed the Chaldean system. Some recorded history also shows the presence of Numerology in China, Rome, Japan and Greece.

Modern numerology has various backgrounds. There are many contributors who have shaped this field in the way it is today. Ruth A. Drayer's book, Numerology, The Power in Numbers states that from the turn of the first century, numerology was mixed with Biblical reference. With the passage of time, many other players came into the field. Dr Jordon in his book "The Romance in Your Name" highlighted the system whereby one could identify the prominent and significant numbers that influences one's name and birth date. These findings still remain an impressive guide for the practitioners across the globe.

WHO WERE THE FATHERS OF NUMEROLOGY, AND WHO HAVE BEEN THE MAJOR CONTRIBUTORS?

Pythagoras, who is well known the world over for his theorem, is referred to as the founding father of Numerology. It is believed that some 2600 years ago in ancient Greece, he laid the stone of numerology. He gave the world the gift of numbers.

He combined the mathematical disciplines of the Arabic, Egyptian, Druid, and Essene and Phoenician sciences. Over the years it has evolved. But in the field of numerology, his style still remains the most followed in the West.

As 20th Century came, many other significant players contributed their knowledge to this field. Prominent amongst them is the American named L. Dow Balliet, along with others initiated the modern phase of numerology. Other significant contributors include:

- Florence Campbell (1931)
- Lynn Buess (1978)
- Mark Gruner (1979)
- Kathleen Roquemore (1985)

Now, in the 21st century, resurgence is being noticed in this field because of the numerous researches and publications. In the present context, you will come across many individuals depending upon numerology to chart up their course of life. As numerology can predict your future, its impact in daily life has become quite significant. You can come across many well known numerologists with a successful track record who will predict your future on the basis of the number chart. People are changing the spelling of their names on the advice of the numerologist so that they can tackle the different obstacles in their life and leave a stress free and tensionless life.

What Can Numerology Do For You

Numerology has significant benefits in our daily life. Although there are many who don't believe in it but an in-depth study of this field will make you aware of its benefits. Over the centuries learned men are relying upon numerology in order to understand how man is in relation to universe – how do both of them exist and become one in the long run. Numerology has been used to understand different happenings across the globe. Different researches have been made to see how the change in numbers might have altered the course of mankind and the different historical events that has shaped the present day life.

Over the different centuries men has been fascinated by how numbers and their relationship with the universe can change the course of our lives. Some of the prominent areas where you can notice the benefits of numerology include:

Know who you are: numerology has the capability to define your traits and characteristics and as such you will be able to know who you are. If go through the different number traits you will see that each number has different and unique characteristics. Now re-read your number! You will be amazed to see that most of your characteristics match with that number. As such you will have a better understanding of your personality and nature. You will come to know about your strengths and weaknesses.

Leap Your Hurdles and Tap Into Your Opportunities:

There will be times when you will find that nothing is working out for you no matter how much you try and then there are times when everything is favorable although you have hardly made any effort. This is because of your Life path number. Knowing your destiny number will prepare you for the future and the different upheavals and as such you will be better prepared to face them.

What is your specialty and carve an individual identity: now that you know your birth number and have calculated your destiny number why don't you carve out a niche for yourself? You are different from others and have your own special characteristics so go on and let the world know your special talents. Why hesitate?

Make the most of your Life's Lessons: in order to enjoy the different life lessons you need to know which the karmic debt numbers are. Generally 4, 5, 7, 13, 14, 16 and 19 are considered to be the Karmic numbers. So go ahead and align yourself with your karmic debt number so as to fully utilize the different lessons and challenges thrown at you so that you evolve in to a better human being.

Find Balance in your life using numbers: the main and purpose of an individual's life is to find balance in anything they do. And in order to attain this balance you need to know your balance number so that you can strive towards a lifestyle where you know how to control your anger, frustration, stress, depression and lead a calm and poised life. The moment you know how to control your temper and the way you express emotions, half of the battle is won.

Know What Your Expression Number Says: in order to arrive at your expression numbers add up your name i.e. add up the corresponding numbers of the alphabets used to spell you name. The single digit that is arrived at the end of the addition is your expression number. And this number is the base of all your skills and abilities.

Determine romance and relationships compatibility: if the numbers are in right order you will experience harmony and co-existence in your relationships. This is applicable in case of both romantic relationships as well as the ones with your friends, family and relatives.

Gain personal insights: numbers can play an interesting game and they can help to reveal the characteristics of an individual. When the different numbers are placed on the chart, the numerologist will tell you what exactly defines you and what your set of principles and beliefs are.

Foresee the future: every month, every year, the life timed cycles change and as such no year is similar to the previous year. But when you have the number chart in front of you, you know how the coming years are going to be and accordingly you can take the precautionary measures.

Life is all about living up to your fullest potential. It is only when that you know yourself in and out that you can handle the obstacles and challenges thrown at you by life. And the main aim of numerology is to help you achieve this mission. Work in accordance with your Life path number in order to make the most of your intellect and potential.

In short numerology is very similar to palmistry in the sense that in both the fields you can predict your future and shape it as well. In one the numbers are used while in the other the fine lines of your palm determine your course of future actions.

How Numerology Works

Numerology is based on mathematical formulas that have remained the same over the years. The underlying theory of numerology is that every name and birth date can be decreased to a single number. And this number becomes the main number on the basis of which your life chart will be created. These numbers are 1, 2, 3, 4, 5, 6, 7, 8, 9, 11, and 22. This single number is arrived at by omitting either the vowels or consonants so that a symbol can be arrived at which is popularly known as the "sigil."

And the numbers that cannot be reduced to a single digit are the master numbers. They are the teachers, builders/architects of the society. The double digit numbers have a higher penchant for life but they tend to experience stress and difficulties in their earthly life. There is one thing here that needs to be taken note of. The master numbers also have a parallel number. Say for example your number is 11 which when added comes to 2. So you will have the characteristics of both the numbers.

With the help of numerology you can easily predict the highs and lows of your life and find out the areas that will help you shine and achieve your dreams. The best part about this field is that it gives you an access to your strengths and weaknesses and provides you with a snapshot of another individual's traits and characteristics.

HOW TO WORK WITH THE NUMBERS, WITH SIMPLE ADDITION, AND SOMETIMES SUBTRACTION

Mastering the art of numerology is like any other skill. The more you practice and use the different tools at your disposal the higher your precision rate will be.

In this field your tools are the numbers itself and the skill lies in suing the numbers to predict the personality and traits of an individual. The more knowledge you have about the different numbers and what they stand for, the higher your ability will be at drawing the life chart. Below we have mentioned in detail the different numbers and their inherent traits so that you can grasp the subject better.

- **The Number One**: Dominant, creative, fame, glory, individualism, male, ambition, aggression, leader, birth, omniscience, alpha, fire, arrogance, self, initiation, fulfillment, unique and happiness, attainment.

- **The Number Two**: grace, female, love, mediation, submissive, harmony, water, dualism, balance, devotion, flexibility, cooperation, adaptability, obedience, consideration, soul mate, the other, dance, adaptability

- **The Number Three**: spontaneity, sex, society, holy trinity, hope, faith, belief, art, triangle, culture, passion, speech, charity, expression, divided, wit, sensuality, immaturity, sorrow, air and change.

- **The Number Four:** Civilization, Commerce, Practical, Foundation, Ability, Traditional, Stability, Wisdom, Conviction, Power, Justice, Conscious Mind.

- **The Number Five**: Adventure, The New Age, Healing, Freedom, Expansion, Story-telling, Mercy, Miracle, Kindness.

- **The Number Six**: Healer, Simplicity, Love of Community, Economy, Balance, Grace, Children, Provider.

- **The Number Seven**: Genius, Chastity, Alchemy, Thinker, Isolation, Analyst, Myth, Religion, Education

- **The Number Eight**: Status, Wealth, Business, Appearance, Reality, Dictatorship, Provision, Riches.

- **The Number Nine**: Religious, Karma, Faith in Mankind, Humanitarian, Suffering, Faith, Wisdom, Duty, Hardship

- **The Number Eleven**: Expression, Alternate Consciousness, Illumination, Intuitive, Psychic, Master Teacher, Poetry, Revolution.

- **The Number Twenty Two**: Ancient Wisdom, the Divine Imagination, Love, Master Builder, Redemption, Realization, Charisma, Service.

As you can see, numerology can be very complex like any human character that has different traits and characteristics. Just like no two individuals are the same way, no two numerological charts will be same. And in order to understand the true characteristics of an individual it takes a lot of calculation that includes the addition of numbers as well as subtractions in order to arrive at the right chart.

How To Do Simple Numerology

In order to understand how numerology works, let us take a number and show you how the whole thing works:

Alex = 1351. Now you need to add up all the different numbers. So the sum total is 1+3+5+1 = 10.
But as per numerology you simply cannot have a number over the digit of 9 hence if you get two numbers after addition you need to add them up further so as to arrive at a single digit. So in this case it will be 1+0 = 1.

By applying simple mathematical formulas one can derive an individual's name as well as the birth date. With these numbers the numerologist can derive his future course of action as well as the 20 to 30 modifiers. When these calculations are done correctly, it will provide a fairly accurate chart of the individual so that it becomes easy to analyze one's character.

HOW TO CONVERT LETTERS OF THE ALPHABET TO NUMBER

Alphabetic systems

Over the years, different societies have come up with t[...] of numerology where they have assigned numbers to dif[...] (of the alphabet). Popular amongst them are:

- Abjad numerals in Arabic
- the Hebrew numerals,
- Armenian numerals
- Greek numerals
- Gematria in Jewish tradition

For example, this is how it works:

1 = a, j, s
2 = b, k, t,
3 = c, l, u,
4 = d, m, v,
5 = e, n, w,
6 = f, o, x,
7 = g, p, y,
8 = h, q, z,
9 = i, r,

Now you need to add up the numbers such as

3,489 → 3 + 4 + 8 + 9 = 24 → 2 + 4 = 6
Hello → 8 + 5 + 3 + 3 + 6 = 25 → 2 + 5 = 7

Abjad system:

Abjad numerals are the creation of the Arabic system and following are the numerical value of the different Arabic alphabets:

أ=1

ب=2

ج=3

د=4

ه=5

و=6

ز=7

ح=8

ط=9

ي=10

ك=20

ل=30

م=40

ن=50

س=60

ع=70

ف=80

ص=90

ق=100

ر=200

ش=300

ت=400

ث=500

خ=600

ذ=700

ض=800

ظ=900

غ=1000

Like this almost each of the languages across the globe has their own numerals and on the basis of that each society has its own numerology through which the characteristics and traits of an individual is calculated.

Note: In the first two chapters we have discussed what is numerology and benefits of numerology. Unless you have grasped the first three chapters, it will be difficult for you to interpret the remaining chapters. Hence it is advisable that you re-read these chapters before proceeding to the remaining chapters.

Meaning of The Numbers

In the previous chapter we have told you that Pythagoras, the famous Greek philosopher is the father of numerology. A mathematician born in the 570 BC, Pythagoras made the world aware of the magic of number. However it was left upon the Mesoamerica to popularize the concept that numbers had spiritual significance and that if the numbers are used carefully then they can make us aware of the happenings around us. IT was left unto the Mayas to impart the knowledge to the rest of the Universe that everything can be broken down to numbers. They were the ones who showed us that numbers were sacred and alive.

The magic of numerology lies on the fact that you need to take your name and the date of your birth in order to achieve the magical single digit number. And the number derived will be the key to your personality. You will get an insight to your inherent traits and characteristics with the help of the particular single digit. Each of the numbers, starting from 1 to 9 has their own unique characteristics and tendencies.

However, true numerology will go a step forward by taking into account the values of all the different numbers of your birthday. All of us have dominant and certain submissive qualities and the numbers will tell you which are the dominant characteristics and which one are the submissive ones. In short it will give you a clear picture of the balanced and imbalanced characteristics.

You can take the calculations a step forward by considering both your name and birth date number. Our names have an inherent power and this is applicable in case of any individual. Our name reveals the hidden clues to our personality. In fact there may be a reason as to why you don't like your name. In this chapter we will discuss about this in detail so that before you proceed to the next chapter you have a clear idea about what the numbers in numerology mean and divulge about us.

Key to Understanding Numerology Meanings:

In numerology, odd numbers represent masculine and even numbers represent feminine. However keep in mind that this masculine or feminine has nothing to do with gender. On the contrary it deals with the masculine and feminine traits present within each individual.

- Masculine: Positive Traits: active, creative. Negative traits: thrusting and cold
- Feminine: Positive traits: receptive, yielding and warm negative traits: passive

The masculine and feminine qualities are within each one of us. In fact you will often come across a guy who is caring and nurturing while a woman is cold and aggressive. These traits are due to the numbers and not because they want to be like that.

As per numerology all the unrest and the dominance of the male gender is due to the shifting tendencies of numbers towards the masculine power. The shift towards balances started approximately about 100 years before when the women's movement started. Majority of the stress, unhappiness and anxiety that is experienced the world over is because of this. Only when the balance is restored and the feminine power restores its lost glory, the world will be balanced. Till then the turmoil will continue.

As already mentioned the numbers in numerology range from 1 to 9 although 11 and 22 also exist. These double digit numbers are known as the master numbers who are associated with the development and shaping of the society. But during calculation the double digits are added and the number achieved is the number used along with the original master number. In other words an individual with the master number will enjoy the traits of both the numbers. The numbers and their meanings are explained in detailed below:

- **The Number One**: Dominant, creative, fame, glory, individualism, male, ambition, aggression, leader, birth, omniscience, alpha, fire, arrogance, self, initiation, fulfillment, unique and happiness, attainment.

- **The Number Two**: grace, female, love, mediation, submissive, harmony, water, dualism, balance, devotion, flexibility, cooperation, adaptability, obedience, consideration, soul mate, the other, dance, adaptability

- **The Number Three**: spontaneity, sex, society, holy trinity, hope, faith, belief, art, triangle, culture, passion, speech, charity, expression, divided, wit, sensuality, immaturity, sorrow, air and change.

- **The Number Four:** Civilization, Commerce, Practical, Foundation, Ability, Traditional, Stability, Wisdom, Conviction, Power, Justice, Conscious Mind.

- **The Number Five**: Adventure, The New Age, Healing, Freedom, Expansion, Story-telling, Mercy, Miracle, Kindness.

- **The Number Six**: Healer, Simplicity, Love of Community, Economy, Balance, Grace, Children, Provider.

- **The Number Seven**: Genius, Chastity, Alchemy, Thinker, Isolation, Analyst, Myth, Religion, Education

- **The Number Eight**: Status, Wealth, Business, Appearance, Reality, Dictatorship, Provision, Riches.

- **The Number Nine**: Religious, Karma, Faith in Mankind, Humanitarian, Suffering, Faith, Wisdom, Duty, Hardship

- **The Number Eleven**: Expression, Alternate Consciousness, Illumination, Intuitive, Psychic, Master Teacher, Poetry, Revolution.

- **The Number Twenty Two**: Ancient Wisdom, the Divine Imagination, Love, Master Builder, Redemption, Realization, Charisma, Service.

NOTE: although we have already discussed this in the previous chapter, but we have again included this in this chapter for a better understanding.

Importance of Name and Birth Date

Now that you know that each number stands for, let us analyze what is the importance of your name that was given to you at your birth. So let us get started.

The first thing that you need to remember is that your birth date is not a single number but the culmination of all the numbers i.e. the day, month and the year. All the numbers have to be added in order to arrive at your numerological number. The number arrived at is referred to as your destiny number because your birth date is not going to change, it is constant. Hence it will determine the course of all your future actions. So let us take a hypothetical number in order to do the calculation.

Let the birth date be 9/12/1984. So the number will be 9+1+2+1+9+8+4 = 34, which when further added will give you 3+4 = 7. (If the number arrived at was a double digit number then you would have to further add it up in order to arrive at a single digit. In other words, you have to go on adding up the numbers until and unless you arrive at a single digit.)

Now that the number arrived at is 7, you need to check the Number7 in order to find out the meaning and personality traits. In other words these are the characteristics of the individual whose birth number we have calculated.

Now let us look at the birthday number. In the example it is 9. Hence this number 9 will also play a significant role in the life of the individual's personality. How the individual behaves and reacts to situation will be guided by this number. This number 9 will also signify the individual's lucky color, month as well as other individuals with whom she will be compatible.

NUMBERS CAN BE USED AS A POSITIVE EXPRESSION, AND AS A NEGATIVE EXPRESSION

If you go through the different number traits (already explained above) you will see that every number ahs both positive and negative traits. In other words you will come to know about both sides of a character of an individual.

Hence the numbers can be used as a positive expression as well as a negative expression. If we take into account the example already cited then the birth number arrive at is 7.

- **The Number Seven**: Genius, Chastity, Alchemy, Thinker, Isolation, Analyst, Myth, Religion, Education

So you see the person is a genius who is also religious minded but prefers isolation and believes in myth. This might pose a problem in the day to day activities and hamper the relations with loved ones as well.

Compare your numerology chart to other personality charts like astrology

Have you ever thought of comparing the numerology chart with you astrology chart? You will be amazed to see the similarities between the two. So does this mean that they are interconnected? Are you curious to learn more about it? Let us take the Mayan astrology for example. The ancient cultures and civilizations were much more refined than ours and the discoveries and calculations made during those times still hold to be true.

If you take into account, the traditional astrology or for that matter the Mayan astrology you will see that both these systems took account of the equinoxes in order to do their calculations. With the advent of the year 2012, the Mayans have predicted that the earth will have a greater opportunity towards spiritual growth than it ever had in recorded history. The earth is entering into the Great Cycle or the Age of Aquarius from this year.

Unique Abilities of The Numbers

The 9 numbers (1 to 9) make up numerology. The entire concept of this field revolves around this number. So far in the previous chapters we have seen how these numbers influence our lives and how each one of us have a specific destiny number. It may happen that more than one individual has the same birth number (after all several hundreds of individuals are born every day of the year). You might come across a colleague or friend who share the same birth number as yours. And this is applicable for each individual across the globe. If you observe carefully, you will see that we have often come across many people who have the same characteristics or traits as us. This is because all these individuals share the same birth number.

Our destiny number plays a significant role in shaping our destiny. The numerologist can easily predict the main incident or events of your life by taking into account this single digit number. However there is one interesting thing to note here. Numerology works not only in case of individuals. It works for different events and incidents occurring across the globe. There are many well known numerologists who have calculated the day, month and year to show why a heinous event took place in a particular year and why the other years were comparatively safe.

Numerology is not only important in the chapters of history but is also very prevalent in the recent context. The World Wide Web is full of different websites where you can type in your birth number and your partner's birth number in order to get an outline of the kind of relationship that you will share. Although there are doubts as to how accurate these sites are, after all they are mechanically monitored but if you visit a numerologist you can ask for your relationship analysis.

Each number in numerology is unique. Each one of them has special characteristics and traits that are different from each other. And each of the numbers has been divided into either masculine or feminine traits. All the different numbers have both positive and negative traits. But ultimately it depends on the individual as to how he will channelize his energy.

(In the third chapter we have explained in detail the different number and their unique characteristics. However for a better understanding, we have shared the same information again.)

- **The Number One**: Dominant, creative, fame, glory, individualism, male, ambition, aggression, leader, birth, omniscience, alpha, fire, arrogance, self, initiation, fulfillment, unique and happiness, attainment.

- **The Number Two**: grace, female, love, mediation, submissive, harmony, water, dualism, balance, devotion, flexibility, cooperation, adaptability, obedience, consideration, soul mate, the other, dance, adaptability

- **The Number Three**: spontaneity, sex, society, holy trinity, hope, faith, belief, art, triangle, culture, passion, speech, charity, expression, divided, wit, sensuality, immaturity, sorrow, air and change.

- **The Number Four**: Civilization, Commerce, Practical, Foundation, Ability, Traditional, Stability, Wisdom, Conviction, Power, Justice, Conscious Mind.

- **The Number Five**: Adventure, The New Age, Healing, Freedom, Expansion, Story-telling, Mercy, Miracle, Kindness.

- **The Number Six**: Healer, Simplicity, Love of Community, Economy, Balance, Grace, Children, Provider.

- **The Number Seven**: Genius, Chastity, Alchemy, Thinker, Isolation, Analyst, Myth, Religion, Education

- **The Number Eight**: Status, Wealth, Business, Appearance, Reality, Dictatorship, Provision, Riches.

- **The Number Nine**: Religious, Karma, Faith in Mankind, Humanitarian, Suffering, Faith, Wisdom, Duty, Hardship

- **The Number Eleven**: Expression, Alternate Consciousness, Illumination, Intuitive, Psychic, Master Teacher, Poetry, Revolution.

- **The Number Twenty Two**: Ancient Wisdom, the Divine Imagination, Love, Master Builder, Redemption, Realization, Charisma, Service.

The Lesson That Each Number Presents

"Life is all memory except for the one present moment that goes by so quick you can hardly catch it going." --Tennessee Williams

Here we will give you an in-depth idea about the different lessons each number represents. In order to make it clear, we will take a life path number and deal with it in detail. Your destiny number has many aspects but most importantly it describes the various lessons of your life that you will experience as you progress in your life. In this chapter we have dealt with this aspect.

By now you already have a clear understanding that your destiny number is the sum total of your birth day, month and year.

Let the birth date be 9/12/1984. So the number will be 9+1+2+1+9+8+4 = 34, which when further added will give you 3+4 = 7. (If the number arrived at was a double digit number then you would have to further add it up in order to arrive at a single digit. In other words, you have to go on adding up the numbers until and unless you arrive at a single digit.)

Honestly, the best way to learn from the different lessons in life is to be awake and aware of the different moments. But that sadly happens. We let our daily routine, fears and memories make up our different moments and as such we fail to live in each moment and thereby end up missing out on the valuable lessons that life has got to offer. In order to learn and grow you need to face life in its daily challenges and overcome them. It is more about being true to yourself which means accepting life as it is and ascertaining your abilities. For all those who rise up to the different challenges that life has to offer, the Life Path number becomes more prominent and guides us in the right direction.

Being able to make use of the different lessons require a level of compassion for others and for yourself. If we analyze the numerous lessons we will see that some of them are inspiring, some distressing and some plain and normal but in short all of them are highly enriching and have shaped us the way we are. Being too hard on yourself will not help much.

Analyzing and understanding your Life Path number will help you find out who you are. In order to discover the real purpose of your life find out the activities that you love to undertake. Unless you have the capacity to learn you will never be able to convert your mistakes to your benefits. The main aim of following the life path number is to listen to your inner voice so that you are peace with yourself. And the trick lies in understanding that it is natural to have fears, anxieties and stress and the main ability lies in accepting them and ensuring that you overcome them.

As we learn more about ourselves the better we are at handling ourselves. In fact you will be better prepared to handle the uncertainties of life. It is important that you learn from your past. However keep in mind that there is a difference between learning from the past and dwelling in the past. Let us take an example. When we were kids we have done many things that we should not have done. Say we have touched a hot stove only to realize that we have burnt the finger. However in the future whenever we are near a hot stove we are careful not to touch it and hence have not burnt our fingers anymore. It is up to us to incorporate what we have learnt in the past. Afterall don't you wish to live a life where mistakes are not a burden but the building blocks to a happy future?

Following are a list of the lessons that are based on the Life Path number.

- **Number One:** individuals with this number should learn to balance independence along with learning how to master self confidence and leadership.

- **Number Two:** Individuals with this number should learn how to share, be optimistic and trust others.

- **Number Three**: if your life path number is three then you need to learn believe in yourself, express and value talents.

- **Number Four**: if this number determines your life then learn to trust others, be non judgmental, have fun after all you cannot control everything.

- **Number five**: start trusting your beliefs, stay in one place so that you can find the time to rest if you have this number as your life path number.

- **Number Six**: if you fall in this number then it is time that you start taking care of yourself, develop personal roles and accept the guilt feelings.

- **Number Seven**: insight, focus and action – these three should be your mantra.

- **Number Eight**: you need to be a good leader and should master the art of sharing responsibilities to others and pay attention to outside opinions for overall growth.

- **Number Nine**: learn to be realistic, trust you gut and avoid isolation if you want your life path number to guide you in the right direction.

- **Number Eleven**: learn to be idealistic.

- **Number Twenty Two**: learn to be practical.

Let us take the life path number 8. If you have this number as your destiny number then you will always have to face situations where you need to make decision. In fact you will have to make sure that the decision is such that it works out well for both you as well as all those who are involved in it. Now you might wonder that all of us face such a situation, so what is so special for people with the number 8 as their life path number? Well individuals with this number have to face such situations repeatedly. As they grow old their decisions will decide the course of their professional and personal life. As such they need to develop a perspective that will help them face these challenges with flying colors.

In order to achieve the balance and make the Life Path number work in favor of you, it is best if you go for meditation. When you are enjoying inner peace and calmness it will be easier for you to handle the outer stress and tension.

Master Numbers

In numerology all the numbers are important but there are three numbers that are extra special and hold a special significance. Those three numbers are 11, 22 and 33. These three numbers are called the "Master Numbers". But what makes them so special that they are termed as the Mater Numbers while the rest are mere numbers?

HOW MASTER NUMBERS ARE OBTAINED, AND WHAT THEY MEAN?

These three Master Numbers have profound implication in one's life and when they are in your chart you can expect some sort of difficulties. But the fact remains that these numbers are not that well understood. Many consider them to be a curse but they can be a blessing as well if you can channelize them in the right way. These numbers can give you an insight on your patience and maturity level as well as a lot of effort in order to peacefully implement all these aspects into your life. And if you can learn to master these numbers then they are the most productive of the lot.

However these master numbers can be reduced to single digit numbers by adding up the two digits. In order to know when you should do this, we have selected this chapter.

Master number 11

The master number 11 stands for instinct and hence is the most intuitive of all the numbers. This number acts as a connection between your subconscious side and your practical side. If you have this number in your chart you will experience strong gut feeling and knowledge and that too without any kind of rationality. If you add up 11 you will get the single digit number 2 and hence will experience all the traits of this number. But keep in mind that the negative traits of 11 are shyness, stressed energy and anxiety. However these are balanced out by the number 2's positive traits like inspiration and charisma. 11 is a dual number hence you will experience both conflict and a dynamic catalism.

One of the biggest drawbacks of the master number 11 is that it gets focused on a specific goal. In case you have this number in your chart and no project is associated with it, you are sure to experience stress and anxiety. This number has great power and has the capability to do things but if not used correctly can be self damaging.

If you want to make the most of this number then you should know how to tap it in order to utilize its true potential. The best way to make the most of this number is to listen to your inner voice so that you are guided by it. Your gut instinct will show you the way towards growth and development. This is a number of faith and belief and is inclined towards the clairvoyants, prophets and physics.

Master number 22

Master number 22 is called the Master Builder as it has more potential than all of the numbers combined and hence they are known by this name. They are considered to be the builders of the society. A pragmatic number, they are capable of turning the wildest of dreams it a happening reality. They are basically doer by nature. Give them an idea and they will make it a reality. If you have this number in your chart then you can expect great success as it has the gut feeling of the master number 11 and enjoys the benefits of the number 4. (When you sum up 22, you get the number 4 right?) Although a highly ambitious number, it is extremely disciplined.

This number stands for lofty goals that can be turned it a reality. However not everyone who has this number enjoys success simply because they have the side effects of both 11 and 22. You will often come across many individuals who have great potential but have somehow never achieved the success – simply because they have this number in their chart. They tend to put unnecessary pressure on themselves.

Master number 33

This number is the real mover and shaker of numerology and hence is referred to as the Master Teacher. But this number occurs very rarely and even when they do most numerologists tend to add them up and reduce it to the single digit 6 thereby minimizing their positive effects.

When you combine the master number 11 and 22 you will get this number. As such people with this number can go much beyond dreams. This number hardly has any agenda and treats humanitarian 0issues as its core. They have a thorough understanding of the project before they take up the project. As such though they are highly knowledgeable they still believe in checking the basic facts to be surer about the project in hand.

HOW MASTER NUMBERS BRING SPECIAL CHALLENGES AND REWARDS

Now that we know what makes these numbers the Master amongst all the numbers in numerology lets us find out what challenges and rewards are brought forward by this number. The energy generated by these numbers is high octane and hence multi dimensional compared to the single digit numbers. As such the energy generated is not run of the mill. They are highly spiritual, unpredictable and are difficult to handle. Individuals with this number experience deeper challenges compared to the rest. They are high on charisma and gain popularity and recognition because of their chosen fields of work. They prefer think out of the box, stay away from the crowd and are often mistaken to be insane and are considered to be notorious.

Master Numbers are often referred to as the "Double Trouble" numbers as it is not easy to live with them. They always have something more to achieve, more Karma to balance even though they have a higher spiritualistic bent of mind then the regular daily affairs. And if you have more than one master number in your chart you will strive for purity in thought and action and intent and anything sort of this will make them restless and experience anxiety.

MASTER NUMBERS CAN MEAN POSSIBLE GREAT THINGS TO COME IN THE FUTURE

The master number 33 is often attributed to be the one that will herald the future. Most of us have an idea or a hunch how the future will turn out to be (Infact many of us are right as well) but those individuals who have the master number 33 in their chart are practically living the future at the present moment. The only problem is that they are deemed unfit and are considered to be avant grade or much ahead than their time. No matter how much they try they can never fit in and there is no harm in it because they are not meant to be.

As the master numbers are the master builder, teacher and messenger of the future they can predict the good things that are going to be there in the future. But the problem lies elsewhere. There are very few individuals who have these master numbers in their chart and as such their characteristics and traits are considered to be not suitable for the present. As well know the past never likes to see itself and as such these master numbers face difficulty from all sides. But as they are the master builder, they are the ones who will shape the future in the most positive way. The teacher will act as a guide and will assist the rest in the right direction.

With the advent of the year 2012, the Mayans have predicted that the earth will have a greater opportunity towards spiritual growth than it ever had in recorded history. The earth is entering into the Great Cycle or the Age of Aquarius from this year.

MASTER NUMBERS - A GIFT OR A CURSE?

Master numbers are highly misunderstood and hence are considered to be a curse. But in reality they are the trend setters. As they appear very rarely in an individual's numerology chart they are considered to be the outsiders. But they are an example of how the future will be. And in the distant future they will appear to be the average normal individual as everyone else surrounding them will be exactly like them.

Individuals with these numbers are blessed with intuition, gut feeling, charisma and the capability to convert dreams into reality. In order to achieve this they tend to put extra pressure on themselves. They need to relax and realize the endless opportunities in front of them. However they always tend to do things in the extreme. As a result if the energy is not channelized it can become a curse and the individual will suffer from extreme anxiety, tension, stress and unpredictable nature. They will get isolated from the crowd and live a life of loneliness. Hence it is extremely important that you channelize your life path number in the right direction.

Conclusion

The art of numerology is based on the characteristics and traits of the numbers, their inherent nature and vibration and how one can use these numbers to better understand themselves and the surrounding world. Most of us never ever thought that even numbers have personality. But by now you know better than that. Let me give you a small example, if you notice carefully you will see that almost all of us have a favorite number, even if they have no idea of numerology. Have you ever wondered why? We make these choices simply because we feel some kind of inner attraction towards them.

Numerology is mainly a self help tool. It is a technique or means of gaining insight to one's character and traits that plays a significant role in defining us. Numerology makes us aware of traits and characteristics that we were completely unaware of. It helps to give a fresh perspective to everything. As a result we tend to see ourselves from a vantage point where we are not influenced by prejudices or judgments. There is no greater tool than self analysis. With this medium you will have a clear understanding of your strengths and weaknesses.

How you will react to the different incidents and scenarios in your life – all will be guided by your birth number. Your birth number is highly detrimental as far as your course of action is concerned. In this book, we have dealt with Numerology in depth so that your concepts are completely cleared and you have a better informed idea about this subject.

Over the different centuries men has been fascinated by how numbers and their relationship with the universe can change the course of our lives. Some of the prominent areas have been discussed in this book for your better grasp of the subject matter.

CPSIA information can be obtained
at www.ICGtesting.com
Printed in the USA
LVHW081046111120
671389LV00013B/345